12 THINGS TO KNOW ABOUT
INVASIVE SPECIES

by Jamie Kallio

www.12StoryLibrary.com

12-Story Library is an imprint of Peterson Publishing Company and Press Room Editions.

Produced for 12-Story Library by Red Line Editorial

Photographs ©: Chris Young/AP Images, cover, 1, 13; Thinkstock, 4, 9, 16, 19, 20; Uriel Garcia/AP Images, 5; Roel Smart/Thinkstock, 6; Roger Alford/AP Images, 7; Heiko Kiera/Shutterstock Images, 8; AP Images, 10, 28; Shutterstock Images, 11, 23, 25, 26; M. Spencer Green/AP Images, 12, 29; Larry D. Hodge/AP Images, 14; Heike Kampe/Thinkstock, 15; David De Lossy/Thinkstock, 17; Paul Maguire/Shutterstock Images, 18; Silvia Letizia Gandolla/Thinkstock, 21; Melinda Fawver/Shutterstock Images, 22; Steve Ruark/AP Images, 24; Photo Fun/Shutterstock Images, 27

ISBN
978-1-63235-030-5 (hardcover)
978-1-63235-090-9 (paperback)
978-1-62143-071-1 (hosted ebook)

Library of Congress Control Number: 2014946810

Printed in the United States of America
Mankato, MN
October, 2014

Go beyond the book. Get free, up-to-date content on this topic at 12StoryLibrary.com.

TABLE OF CONTENTS

PEOPLE SPREAD INVASIVE SPECIES

Invasive species are a worldwide problem. A plant, animal, or microorganism species that thrives in an area outside its normal territory is called invasive. It does not belong there. Invasive species can cause great harm. They compete with other species for food, shelter, and other natural resources. Most have been introduced by humans.

Historically, humans have introduced invasive species while traveling or exploring. Sometimes they brought species with them on purpose. Early colonists to North America carried plants, seeds, and animals from Europe. Such species include cows and horses. Other plants, animals, insects, and microorganisms hid in crates. They were accidentally introduced to North America.

Asian tiger mosquitos were introduced to the United States by accident.

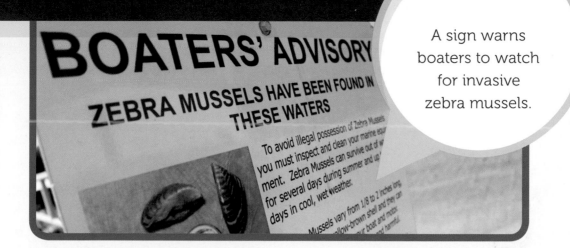

BOATERS' ADVISORY

ZEBRA MUSSELS HAVE BEEN FOUND IN THESE WATERS

To avoid illegal possession of Zebra Mussels you must inspect and clean your marine equipment. Zebra Mussels can survive out of water for several days during summer and up to days in cool, wet weather.

Mussels vary from 1/8 to 2 inches long, yellow-brown shell and they can ... ur boat and motor ... d harmful.

A sign warns boaters to watch for invasive zebra mussels.

Today humans continue to introduce invasive species, both on purpose and by accident. Some, such as the kudzu vine, were introduced to provide food for animals and humans. Others, such as the Burmese python, were brought into their new habitats as pets. When they escape or are released, they cause problems for other species. Humans try to manage invasive species. They may physically remove them. Or they may use chemicals or other species to kill the invasive species.

4,300
Invasive species currently in the United States.

- Early colonists brought many invasive species to their new homes.
- Invasive species alter habitats by competing with native plants and animals.
- Invasive species can be pets that have escaped or been released into the wild.

THE EARLIEST INVADERS

Humans were the first species to spread outside of their original territory. Humans first emerged from Africa 50,000 to 70,000 years ago. Gradually, they spread across the globe. Early humans brought invasive species with them. They brought possums and dogs to Indonesia. They introduced dingoes to Australia.

KUDZU IS THE VINE THAT ATE THE SOUTH

Kudzu is a climbing vine native to Asia. People eat its roots and use its stems to make fibers. It has been used for thousands of years as medicine, too.

Kudzu was introduced to the United States at the 1876 Philadelphia Centennial Exposition. It was promoted as a decorative plant and as livestock feed. In the 1930s, farmers in the South used kudzu as ground cover to help prevent soil erosion. By the mid-1940s, kudzu had been planted on 1.2 million acres (486,000 ha).

Kudzu is fast growing and spreads quickly. It can grow up to 1 foot (30 cm) per day. Its thick roots can

The kudzu vine covers everything in its path.

Scientists try to control kudzu with chemicals.

extend 12 feet (3.7 m) into the soil and weigh up to 400 pounds (181 kg). The roots can store a lot of water. The plant is very hardy and can survive in both sun and shade. However, it thrives best in full sun and warm temperatures. That is why it grows especially well in the South. After farmers used it to prevent erosion, it quickly started taking over. It overruns anything in its path. Since it is a climbing vine, kudzu can cover trees and telephone poles. Places that are abandoned or neglected are especially at risk. Kudzu crowds out other plants for space and nutrients. If left to grow, the vine is very difficult to destroy. People call kudzu "the green menace" and the "mile-a-minute vine." They also call it "the vine that ate the South."

100

Length, in feet, that a kudzu vine can grow.

- Kudzu was brought to the United States as a decorative plant and for livestock food.
- It was used in the South to battle soil erosion.
- Kudzu has extremely strong, deep roots.
- The plant has many nicknames, including "the vine that ate the South."

BURMESE PYTHONS ARE PREDATORS OF PREDATORS

The Burmese python is one of the world's largest snakes. It can grow to be more than 23 feet (7 m) long. Some weigh as much as 200 pounds (91 kg). They are native to the jungles and marshes of Southeast Asia. But now Burmese pythons can be found in southern Florida. They are especially common in Everglades National Park.

People keep Burmese pythons as pets. But they often grow too large for their owners to properly care for them. Many of these snakes either escape or are released into the wild. Burmese pythons released into cool regions rarely survive. But the Florida Everglades are warm and wet like the pythons' native habitat. The snakes there are able to survive and breed. In 2011 scientists estimated there were between 30,000 and 100,000 Burmese pythons in the Everglades.

A Burmese python that has made its home in the Everglades

152

Number of Burmese pythons removed from Everglades National Park and the surrounding areas in 2012.

- Burmese pythons are one of the largest snakes in the world.
- Reptile owners often find they can no longer care for their adult Burmese pythons.
- Burmese pythons either escape or are intentionally released into the wild.
- There are between 30,000 and 100,000 Burmese pythons living in the Everglades.

THINK ABOUT IT

Pets such as the Burmese python can become invasive species if released into the wild. Do you have any pets at home? Is there a type of pet that you would like to own? Research your pet or a pet you would like. List the ways it could help or harm the environment if released into the wild.

Burmese pythons pose a problem for Florida. They cause damage to the ecosystem. No other animal hunts and eats them. But the pythons eat other species. Scientists believe they will drastically decrease the number of Florida's native species. They have been known to eat full-grown deer and even alligators. The snakes also compete with native predators, such as the Florida panther, for food.

Though predators themselves, alligators can be prey for the Burmese python.

INTRODUCING KILLER BEES WAS A SERIOUS ERROR

Killer bees are the result of an experiment gone wrong. In 1956 researchers wanted to improve beekeeping in the tropics. European bees did not thrive in warm temperatures. The researchers brought bees from Africa to Brazil.

They bred them with European honey bees to create a hybrid. The researchers hoped to create a bee that would produce more honey. What they created was the Africanized honey bee.

WHY "KILLER"?

Africanized honey bees have earned the nickname "killer bees." But individual bees are not killers. In fact, Africanized honey bees have the same amount of venom as ordinary honey bees. However, Africanized honey bees attack in swarms rather than as individuals. That means victims receive more stings—and more bee venom.

Africanized honey bees are more aggressive than European honey bees.

30

Average length, in days, of a worker bee's lifespan.

- Africanized honey bees were developed in 1957 in Brazil.
- Now they can be found in Central and North America.
- Africanized honey bees are very aggressive.
- Beekeepers are developing ways to deal safely with Africanized honey bees.

The Africanized honey bee thrived in tropical Brazil. In 1957 26 Africanized queen bees escaped their hives. They spread north and began to breed with local bees. Their offspring were found in Mexico in 1985. By 1990 the so-called killer bees had swarmed to Texas, Arizona, and California.

Africanized honey bees cause many problems. They often take over the hives of regular bees. Killer bees are much more aggressive than other bees, which makes them difficult for beekeepers to control. Swarms will attack if a person or animal gets too close to the bees' nest. They keep stinging until they drive the threat away. Some people have died from killer bee stings.

Beekeepers have learned new skills to deal with Africanized honey bees. One strategy is to keep bee colonies separate to lessen swarming behavior. Beekeepers also use lots of smoke when working with the hybrid bees. The smoke calms the bees.

Beekeepers use smoke to keep killer bees calm.

5

INVASIVE ASIAN CARP ARE EATING MACHINES

Imagine a 4-foot (1.2 m) long fish leaping out of a lake into a boat. Now imagine that fish is 100 pounds (45 kg). It is not a monster. It is the Asian carp, an invasive species.

Asian carp is a name used to describe four species of fish. The silver, bighead, grass, and black carp are from Southeast Asia. All eat by straining little pieces of food from water. The fish can eat up to 20 percent of their body weight every day. They were introduced into the United States in the 1970s. Fish farmers in Arkansas used them to filter water on their farms. But flooding allowed them to escape into wild waters. They began reproducing.

Since their escape, Asian carp have spread quickly up the Mississippi River and connecting rivers. They have big appetites. Asian carp compete with native fish species for food. They primarily eat plankton, tiny animals at the bottom of the food chain. Many other species also eat plankton. Asian carp eat so much that other fish are in danger of dying out. Carp have destroyed underwater vegetation in many

Asian carp compete with other fish for food.

rivers. This vegetation provided habitats for many native fish and other living creatures.

Asian carp have no natural predators to help control their numbers. This makes them almost impossible to get rid of. Today Asian carp are found in the waters of 23 states. Wildlife officials are determined to keep them from spreading up the Illinois River and into the Great Lakes. The Army Corps of Engineers built an electrical barrier to keep the fish out. It is on the canal connecting the Illinois River to Lake Michigan. Scientists hope this barrier will keep the carp out of Lake Michigan. They hope it will give them time to develop other ways to fight the fish.

$7 billion

Worth of the Great Lakes' sport and commercial fisheries threatened by an Asian carp invasion.

- Asian carp is the name given to four species of invasive fish.
- The carp eat up to 20 percent of their body weight in a day.
- Their main diet is plankton, which other fish species also eat.
- Scientists are developing ways to prevent the fish from spreading up the Mississippi River.

Asian carp jump up to 10 feet (3 m) when startled.

ZEBRA MUSSELS THRIVE IN POLLUTED WATERS

Zebra mussels are only about 1 inch (2.5 cm) long. But their ability to upset native ecosystems is enormous. Normally, freshwater mussels are good animals to have in lakes and rivers. They clean the water they live in as they eat. Most are very sensitive. They suffer if their water becomes disturbed or too polluted. But zebra mussels seem to thrive in polluted waters.

Zebra mussels get their name from the dark, striped pattern on their shells. Their native habitat is the waters of the Caspian and Black Seas in central Asia. They were found in Lake St. Clair, Michigan, in 1988. Scientists believe zebra mussels arrived in the United States in water dumped from large European ships. Since then, they have spread rapidly through the Great Lakes. They also can be found in the Mississippi, Tennessee, Cumberland, Ohio, Arkansas, and Illinois Rivers. They attach themselves to most man-made materials, including boats.

Zebra mussels breed quickly. They colonize inside pipes that deliver water to

Zebra mussels line a water pipe.

cities and power plants. They cling to every inch of space. When no pipe is left, they attach to one another, clogging the pipe. They even attach in large quantities to native mussels. As many as 10,000 zebra mussels have attached to just one native mussel. This eventually kills the native mussels.

Algae blooms can choke out plants and animals living in lakes and ponds.

Scientists fear zebra mussels are harming freshwater lakes. They avoid eating the bacteria that cause algae to bloom. Algae can make it difficult for animals to breathe and other plants to survive. Scientists have developed different methods to remove or decrease the numbers of zebra mussels. These methods include removal by hand or using chemicals and electrical currents.

600

Estimated number of lakes and reservoirs in the United States invaded by zebra mussels.

- European ships accidentally brought zebra mussels to the United States.
- Zebra mussels thrive in both clean and polluted water.
- Once they attach themselves to a hard surface, zebra mussels are difficult to remove.
- Zebra mussels can be found in the Great Lakes and many major rivers.

BLACK RATS CARRIED THE BLACK DEATH

Black rats caused the deaths of 25 million people between 1347 and 1352 CE. They carried fleas that spread the Black Death. The Black Death was another name for the bubonic plague, an infectious disease. The Black Death spread rapidly across Europe. The fleas that bit the rats also bit humans, spreading the disease. The Black Death killed a third of Europe's population. Today bubonic plague in the United States is rare. Doctors can treat it using antibiotics.

Black rats probably originated in Southeast Asia. They spread to other countries along the trade routes between Asia and Europe. In the 1500s, they appeared in Central and South America. They were aboard the ships from Europe arriving in Jamestown, Virginia, in 1610.

Black rats carried fleas that infect humans with the Black Death.

7

Number of continents on which the black rat is found.

- Black rats were the carriers of bubonic plague, or Black Death.
- They spread through the world on ships and along trade routes.
- Black rats can harm native species.
- Rat-proofing homes and securing pet food can help prevent rats from making a nest.

THINK ABOUT IT

Black rats carried Black Death, or bubonic plague. What other diseases do rodents carry? Use one or two more sources to research this question.

The Invasive Species Specialist Group named the black rat as one of the 100 "World's Worst" invaders. Black rats tend to live in warm areas close to humans. They prefer to nest indoors in attics and rafters. This is why the Black Death infected so many people so quickly. The rats have also killed off some native species in their adopted homelands. They threaten native species by eating their young or their eggs. In the 1880s in Hawaii, they caused the extinction of the honeycreeper songbird. They currently threaten other native seabirds, such as Bonin petrels.

To manage black rats, humans must stop colonies from forming. They can rat-proof roofs and clear out overgrown plants and shrubs. This will get rid of places for the rats to live. People can keep pet food secure so rats do not get into it. Rat poison can also be used, but it is very toxic.

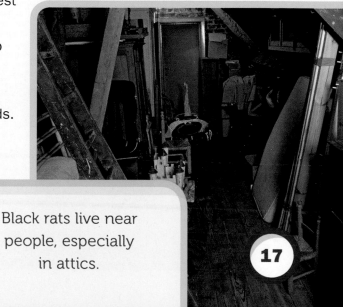

Black rats live near people, especially in attics.

8

THE EUROPEAN RABBIT INVADED AUSTRALIA

The cute, little European rabbit is actually one of the world's most invasive species. It was brought to Australia in the mid-nineteenth century. Since then, the rabbits have overrun most of the country. They have caused great damage to Australia's agriculture and environment. The European rabbit is a good example of the dangers of invasive species.

The European rabbit originated in North Africa and spread north to Italy. From there, the species spread to the British Isles and around the world. After 12 pairs of them were released on an Australian ranch in the 1800s, rabbit numbers exploded. There were no natural predators of rabbits in Australia. By 1953 rabbits numbered in the several hundred millions.

They may be cute, but European rabbits are pests in Australia.

Rabbits only eat plants. In Australia, they have caused much damage to the environment. They eat grass used for raising sheep. They destroy large numbers of native plants and wildlife. Their grazing threatens birds, insects, and other animals that eat and live in the plants. The rabbits' underground homes have caused soil problems.

Efforts to control the rabbits in Australia have had mixed results. Some people inject poisons into the rabbits' homes. Others have introduced predators, such as feral cats, to try to cut back their numbers. Some scientists tried introducing a virus that targeted only rabbits. Other scientists, however, were concerned the virus could attack other species. The latest data estimates that the number of rabbits has decreased. From 200 to 300 million rabbits, their population is down to about 100 million. However, the rabbits breed very often. The rabbits in Australia are in no real danger of dying out for good.

> Some Australians rely on feral cats to control rabbit numbers.

12

Number of pairs of European rabbits originally released in Australia in the 1800s.

- By 1953 in Australia, rabbits numbered in the hundred millions.
- They destroyed the plants other species relied on for food and shelter.
- Humans have tried to control their numbers with poison, feral cats, and a virus.

THE CANE TOAD IS TOXIC TO PREDATORS

At 4 to 6 inches (10 to 15 cm) long, cane toads are some of the largest toads in the world. It is native to Central America. Cane toads were brought to Hawaii and other parts of the world in the 1930s. They were brought to help control sugarcane beetles. The cane toads adapted well to their new homes. They now number in the millions in North America and Australia.

Cane toads have large glands on top of their heads that contain

Cane toads are poisonous pests.

Honey bees can become prey for cane toads.

poison. The poison can kill animals that try to eat the toads. With their poison as protection, the cane toads spread throughout their new homes quickly. Cane toads are meat-eaters. They eat insects, small mammals, snakes, lizards, and frogs. The toads are also tough. Most toads need to stay moist to survive. A cane toad can survive losing up to half of the water in its body. It can also survive in extremely cold temperatures.

Today cane toads are abundant. They are a toxic danger to pets who try to eat them. They are harmful to the humans who may touch them. Their large appetites cause them to compete with native species for food. They eat honey bees, which causes problems for bee keepers and honey production. They may also carry diseases that infect native frogs and fish.

There has been no simple way to control the spread of cane toads. Removing cane toad eggs from bodies of water sometimes works.

Another strategy is to try and keep the toads away from water sources in the hope that they will dry out and die.

$2.3 million

Estimated amount the Australian government spent from 2008 to 2011 on a cane toad removal plan.

- Cane toads have glands on the tops of their heads that release a poison.
- They will eat almost anything.
- They compete with native species for food and are extremely hardy.
- People have tried several tactics to keep cane toad numbers down.

ASIAN TIGER MOSQUITOS ARRIVED IN TIRES

Originally from tropical Southeast Asia, the Asian tiger mosquito most likely arrived in Hawaii after World War II (1939–1945). They first appeared in the continental United States in Houston, Texas, in 1985. Since then they have spread to the southeastern United States, Europe, the Caribbean, Africa, and the Middle East. According to the Global Invasive Species Database, the Asian tiger mosquito is one of world's worst invasive species.

In the 1980s, tires from Asia were being imported into the United States. The Asian tiger mosquito hitched a ride in tires from Japan. Asian tiger mosquitos are aggressive. They will bite humans, squirrels, dogs, deer, and livestock. They are carriers of many diseases, including West Nile Virus and yellow fever.

So far, the best way to manage the Asian tiger mosquito is to remove any potential breeding sites. People discard or dump out old tires, tin cans, buckets,

Asian tiger mosquitos have black and white stripes on their legs and bodies.

10

Number of times the Asian tiger mosquito can bite the same person.

- The Asian tiger mosquito most likely arrived in Hawaii after World War II.
- The insect is now found in the southeastern United States, Europe, the Caribbean, Africa, and the Middle East.
- The mosquito is resistant to many insecticides.

WATERY NURSERIES

Mosquitos breed any time from the beginning of spring to the first hard frost of autumn. After a few days of feeding on blood, the female mosquito lays her eggs. She lays them just above the surface of the water in any container. A bucket, tire, gutter, or even a hole in a tree can be ideal spots. When rain covers the eggs with water, the larvae hatch.

and other containers that hold water. Unfortunately, the tiger mosquito is resistant to many insecticides. But insecticides can kill the larvae.

Since 1988 the US government has required used tires from areas with the Asian tiger mosquito to be cleaned.

Old tires make good mosquito nurseries.

NORTHERN SNAKEHEAD FISH CAN LIVE ON LAND, TOO

Northern snakeheads are freshwater fish originally from China, North Korea, and Russia. There are 28 species of snakehead fish. Some colorful ones are popular in aquariums. But the northern snakehead is not one of these pretty fish. The large scales on its flat head make it look like a snake. It can grow about 3 feet (1 m) long and weigh up to 15 pounds (6.8 kg). It has a large mouth filled with shark-like teeth.

In some parts of Asia, people eat the northern snakehead. Northern snakehead fish were brought to North America as food. They were first sighted in Silverwood Lake, California, in 1977. In 2002 they were discovered in Crofton, Maryland. They have since spread to Virginia.

Not many people would choose to put a northern snakehead in an aquarium.

Northern snakeheads often make a meal of smaller fish.

Female snakeheads can spawn up to 15,000 eggs five times a year. This is more than many other fish species. As with most invasive species, the northern snakehead competes with native species for food and living space. Northern snakeheads are carnivores. They eat large amounts of fish and frogs. They also eat small reptiles, birds, and even mammals. They prefer to live in shallow, muddy ponds or wetlands. Though they like warmer water, the fish can live under ice, too. The northern snakehead can even breathe air and wriggle across land. This helps them reach other bodies of water. They can survive on land for up to four days.

It is hard to manage such a hardy fish species without killing native fish. Since 2002 federal law has banned the transport of live northern snakeheads into the United States. The law may prevent new introductions of the fish.

90

Percentage of the northern snakehead's diet that consists of other fish.

- Northern snakehead is a food delicacy in parts of Asia.
- The fish can breathe air and crawl across land.
- Snakeheads prefer warm temperatures but can survive under ice.

THINK ABOUT IT

Compare the northern snakehead fish to the Asian carp. Which fish do you think is more destructive? Use facts about both to support your opinion.

THE COST OF INVASIVE SPECIES IS HIGH

Many ecologists believe the threat of invasive species is one of the world's biggest problems. They worry that invasive species will cause long-standing ecosystems to fall apart. These non-native invaders stand to alter biodiversity.

Biodiversity is the variety of plants, animals, and other living things in an ecosystem. Humans are included in this system. Every type of plant and animal has a specific role. Plants, animals, and insects rely on each other for survival. Invasive species upset the ecosystem.

Ecosystems include all the living things on land and in the water.

$314 billion

Amount invasive species cost the United States, the United Kingdom, Brazil, Australia, South Africa, and India in 2008.

- Ecologists believe invasive species are one of the world's biggest problems.
- Invasive species alter ecosystems and harm biodiversity.
- Out-of-control invasive species do great damage and cost the world billions each year.

destroyed about 10 percent of cattle grazing lands. It has cost Brazil's economy about $30 million per year. Invasive insects in the United Kingdom cause an estimated $3.7 billion per year in crop losses. Invasive species do a lot of damage. Efforts continue worldwide to help stop or decrease the negative impacts of invasive species.

The harlequin ladybird causes crop losses in the United Kingdom.

Out-of-control invasive species ruin crops, interfere with businesses, and spread disease. They kill native plants and animals. They require large amounts of time and money to control. In the United States in 2008, invasive species cost the economy between $120 billion and $140 billion. In Brazil an invasive type of plant called lovegrass has

FACT SHEET

- Invasive species are a worldwide problem. The term "invasive species" is given to any plant, animal, or microorganism that has invaded an area outside of its normal territory. Not all invasive species thrive in their new environments. When they do thrive, they often cause great harm by altering habitats. The cost of invasive species in some of the world's largest nations is estimated at $314 billion each year.

- Both plants and animals can be invasive species. Kudzu is a climbing vine that was brought to the United States in the 1880s. Now it is known as "the vine that ate the South." Aggressive Africanized honey bees were first bred in Brazil. Today they are found in Central and North America.

- Many species that live in water can be invasive. Asian carp is the name given to four species of fish that have found their way to the Great Lakes. Once the Asian carp establishes itself in an environment, it is almost impossible to remove. Zebra mussels come from the harsh waters of the Caspian and Black Seas. They now live in lakes and rivers in the United States.

- Invasive species can carry diseases that affect other animals, as well as humans. Black rats were carriers of the bubonic plague, otherwise known as the Black Death. Twenty-five million people died as a result. Cane toads have poisonous glands on their heads that can harm humans.

GLOSSARY

compete
To be in rivalry with someone or something.

ecologists
Scientists who study the relationships between groups of living things and their environments.

ecosystem
All living and non-living things in a particular area.

gland
An organ in the body that produces or releases natural chemicals.

hybrid
Something created when two or more forms are combined.

larvae
A very young form of an insect.

microorganism
An extremely small living thing that can only be seen with a microscope.

native
Living or growing naturally in a particular region.

reproduce
To produce offspring.

soil erosion
A process that occurs when wind or water washes or blows away the top layer of dirt.

species
A group of animals or plants that are similar and can reproduce.

FOR MORE INFORMATION

Books

Jackson, Cari. *Alien Invasion: Invasive Species Become Major Menaces.* Pleasantville, NY: Gareth Stevens, 2010. Print.

Metz, Lorijo. *What Can We Do About Invasive Species?* New York: PowerKids, 2010. Print.

O'Connor, Karen. *The Threat of Invasive Species.* New York: Gareth Stevens, 2014. Print.

Websites

Eek! Alien Invaders. Environmental Education for Kids
www.dnr.wi.gov/org/caer/ce/eek/earth/aliens.htm

Invasive Species. National Geographic Education
www.education.nationalgeographic.com/education/encyclopedia/invasive-species/?ar_a=1

Invasive Species. National Wildlife Federation
www.nwf.org/Wildlife/Threats-to-Wildlife/Invasive-Species.aspx

INDEX

About the Author

Jamie Kallio is a youth services librarian in the south suburbs of Chicago, Illinois. She is the author of many nonfiction titles for children. When she is not busy researching, she is hanging out with her husband, dog, and three cats.